Mary Macalpine

The Traitor Lake

And Other Poems

Mary Macalpine

The Traitor Lake
And Other Poems

ISBN/EAN: 9783744695985

Printed in Europe, USA, Canada, Australia, Japan

Cover: Foto ©Thomas Meinert / pixelio.de

More available books at **www.hansebooks.com**

THE TRAITOR LAKE,

AND OTHER POEMS.

BY

MARY MACALPINE.

GREENOCK:
W. HUTCHISON, 23 NICOLSON STREET.
1895.

DEDICATION.

CONTENTS.

	Page
DEDICATION	v.
THE TRAITOR LAKE	1
THE LEGEND OF THE CHRISTMAS ROSE	15
THE STORY OF ERIC	21
WHY?	35
WHICH?	39
FIAMMETTA	43
MARY LEE	51
AMOR MORTUUS	57
SONG—MY LOVE WHO LOVES ME NOT	61
TWIN SOULS	65
MOONLIGHT ON COMO	69
THE LOVE BIRD	75
A PERFECT DAY	79
LUX ET TENEBRAE	83
FROM THE ITALIAN OF STECCHETTI	87
AFTER STECCHETTI	91
SOMEWHERE	95
AFTER MANY DAYS	101

THE TRAITOR LAKE.

The Traitor Lake.

PROLOGUE.

LAND of the olive and vine, of the myrtle, the sweet oleander;
Land of the snowy magnolia lading the air with its perfume;
(Flowers so heavenly fair, that fain would we dream and imagine
One day they grew in the lost, in the mythical garden of Eden);
Land of the sapphire skies, whose depths of ethereal blueness
Burn in the waters below them, in stillness and azure reflections.

Land of the glorious sun, of the soft evening
    breezes in summer,
Tinting the clear pallid skins and wooing the
    hearts of the people!
Land of the thunder and storms which resound
    in the loves of the people,
Leaving a mark, as of flame, with their influence
    ever upon them!
Take from the hand of a stranger this tribute
    of grateful devotion—
Take these her words and the story of one of thy
    sons as she heard it;
(Told in a tongue inharmonious, perhaps, to the
    ear of the Latins);
Take this poor verse from her heart. Italia,
    Here I salute thee!

Fair shone the waters of Como, this day of
    the Holy Ascension,

Girt like some deep-set pearl by the sky-dwelling peaks of the mountains.
Quiet the village lay in the hush of the calm summer morning,
Only the clanging of bells from the grey and the red of the belfry
Called the believers to prayer, to the duties, the Mass of the Festa.
Here, on the lake's still bosom, I rocked to the throb and the murmurs,
Heard in an undertone from the depth of the sobbing of waters,
Answered in turn by the bells of the fishing nets under the wavelets.
Listening now to the tinkling, and now to the crooning of music,
Rising and falling like bells in the voice of my little companion:
Chaunting in time and in rhyme, to the scarce-defined ebb and the rocking,

Some ancient hymn of her church for this Feast of the Holy Ascension.

Drifting we seemed in a dream, when at length my little companion

Suddenly ceased in her singing, and raising herself on her elbow,

Pointed her hand to the shore, to the rocks which now towered above us,

Pointed to where I could see on the cliffs forty feet o'er the water

Resting, a marble slab, by garlands of roses encircled,

Blossoms so fresh that last eve, at the latest, they surely were gathered.

Marta, with eyes gazing upwards, and fixed on the block of Carrara,

Crossing her tiny bosom, now turned with her face full of sorrow,

"See, oh Signora," she said, "they have brought them these beautiful roses!

Showing poor Tito, and Nino, and Paolo they are not forgotten."
Then in the slow-rocking boat just under the marble and flowers,
Marta, with tears in her eyes and her voice, here told me the pitiful story :—

" On the last Feast of Ascension, just after the hot mezzo-giorno
Had faded a little to coolness, then Tito, and Nino, and Paolo,
All in their festival clothes, with sashes of blue and of scarlet,
Rowed to the opposite shore, to fetch a young man to the dancing,
Carlo, the best of the dancers, the boatman beloved of Guidita.
Only our Tito was pale, and we saw that his heart was on fire.

Jealous of all men was he, but jealous the most
of poor Carlo,
So, while with a jest and a laugh, all the others
saluted Guidita,
He turned his face to the lake, and the boat shot
out over to Blevio.

"Hardly two hours were gone when we saw o'er
the Switzerland mountains
Creeping up slowly a cloudlet, that stained the
bright belts of the heavens.
Then ran the fishermen down to the shore where
the boats were all lying,
Dragging them up on the beach, while the first
distant rumble of thunder
Shook in the far-off air, and the swallows flew
low o'er the water.
Soon, by the side of the lake, the mothers and
daughters were gathered,

THE TRAITOR LAKE.

Telling each other to fear not the storm, which would quickly blow over;
And, at the worst, the young men were the bravest and best of all boatmen,
All the three skilled at the oar, and all trained to the rudder in steering,
Knowing the winds and the currents, the waves of the 'Lake Traditore.'

"But, as the clouds grew denser we heard the beginning of moaning
Up in the mountain forest, through boughs of the oak and the pine-trees;
People in larger numbers hurried now down to the lake-side,
Nearest of all stood Guidita; her face was as pale as a lily;
And twisted around her fair neck was a kerchief of Carlo's own colour.

" Down came the winds from the Alps, and the waters upheaving
Thundered and crashed in the lake. In a moment the mist and the darkness
Hid from our eyes the sharp line of the opposite mountains of Blevio.
Then came a lull in the tempest, and lo! on the waving of waters,
Just half-way over we saw (how we shuddered and shivered in seeing)
Oh! such a frail little boat as it seemed in that rush of wild weather.
And then we all knew on the wind-driven lake tossed our men and that other
With fathers and mothers on shore in a frenzy of helpless inaction!

" One moment a dozen large barks were launched out with a will to the rescue,

When down came the whirlwind again with its horrible hissing and darkness.
And then, with a shriek, poor Guidita fell prone by the side of her mother,
Twisting the silk at her throat, and moaning her lover, 'Poor Carlo!'"

There was a pause for a moment, and Marta, with face half-averted,
Echoed the last of her words, and the rocks seemed to whisper 'Poor Carlo!'
And then the slow lapping of water, the sobbing of waves seemed to answer,
All mixed with sighs from my heart in the dirge of that echo for 'Carlo.'

But now in a moment the maiden resuming the tale of the tempest :—

"Ah! 'twas not he that was lost, for Guidita is married to Carlo.
They knew—the first boatman who neared them, 'twas life for the one or the other,
When, thrusting the last floating oar 'neath the arms of the struggling Carlo,
Brave Tito sank down for her sake. Our Tito; *he chose for Guidita.*
And theirs are the hands, while they live, that shall gather these beautiful roses
For Tito, and Nino, and Paolo—but weeping they weave them for Tito.
'Tis they who shall keep, oh Signora, this Feast of the Holy Ascension
In Church, as a day of sad mourning, of fasting, of prayers, and of masses,
For the good of the soul of brave Tito—that none of his friends may forget him."

EPILOGUE.

Land of the sun and the flowers, the wonders of storms and of tempests,
Land of the Traitor Lake, with its smiles, its reflections of heaven!
Take from the hand of a stranger this tribute of grateful devotion,
(Told in a tongue inharmonious, perhaps, to the ear of the Latins)—
Tribute to thee and thy son for the lesson his story has taught her,
Take this poor verse from her heart. Italia, Here I salute thee.

THE LEGEND
OF THE CHRISTMAS ROSE.

The Legend of the Christmas Rose.

Dark fell the night on which our Lord was born
   In that rude manger of far Bethlehem;
When shepherds came to worship at His shrine—
   Stayed by the star, which staying guided them.
And with them bearing many precious things
Came from afar the three great Magi Kings.

The shepherds by their flocks had seen the star,
   Had heard the angel-chorus in the night,
The heavenly message "Peace on earth; goodwill
   To men," had echoed from the spangled height.
And, following them, in wondering humbleness,
Came little Madelon, the shepherdess.

Came to adore the Infant Christ; but now
    They went into that stall so rude and dim,
While still she stood outside with breaking heart
    And falling tears, she had no gift for Him.
I am so poor! So cold the north wind blows;
If I could gather but a single rose!"

The spring is yet so very far away;
    The roses all are dead, long, long ago;
The frost is keen; I dare not enter in;
    Dear God, I am so poor; I love Him so!"
When round about there flashed a radiance bright,
And lo! an Angel stood within the light!

It was the Angel Gabriel from heaven,
    Who hears the children crying on the earth;
When God's great hosts were singing, he had come
    To learn who wept at the dear Saviour's birth.
"Why do you weep? oh! little shepherdess;
Why do you pray?" he asked, with tenderness.

"Alas!" sobbed Madelon, with quavering voice,
   "They have gone in with gifts; I have no rose—
Not even a flower to offer to the Babe;
   It freezes hard, and cold the north wind blows.
Therefore I weep alone, I have no store—
I must stay here without for evermore!"

Summer is gone, and spring is far away,
   Autumn's dead leaves lie covering the land;
Good Angel, woe is me!" But Gabriel smiled
   Down on poor Madelon; then took her hand,
And answering her—"Thy prayer is heard of God,"
He struck the frozen earth beneath his rod—

A miracle! It blossomed into flowers,
   And Madelon the roses plucked amazed.
Thanking the Angel; but the light grew dim
   While Gabriel vanished slowly as she gazed.
Oh, joy! she entered at the stable-door
And laid the Angel's gift the babe before!

This is the Legend of the Christmas Rose.
And we, like Madelon the shepherdess,
Can always pray to Him who came this night
On earth to help us in our bitterness.
What, though our hearts be sad, our eyes be dim,
Some love-flowers we may always give to Him!

THE STORY OF ERIC.

The Story of Eric.

EXPECTATION.

Our cottage had a garden skirting down
Right to the sea-sands; nothing rose between
Our latticed windows and the wild wide sky,
And God Almighty's waters, and his grand
Great pictures—of the dewy smiling morns,
Of scarlet sunsets, and the changing tints
Of every hour in all the live-long day.

When Eric sailed—just as the freshening winds
Were blowing from the north—the roses died.
But now I stood 'mid all the wealth of June,
'Neath glinting rays of sunshine falling there,

Bathing each leaf in amber-tinted light;
And all the wandering winds that stirred the air
Sang music to a happy singing heart
In June's fair noontide.

                      He was coming home.
The ship "Abundance" had been hailed at sea
By one of our great vessels, then we heard
That she had passed the Lizard, perhaps to-day
Would see her coming with her great sails set,
Grey-winged upon the waters, into port.

Ah, dear my sailor lad, whose handsome face
Must be so reddened by the healthy wind,
I think I see you lifting up the latch,
Then hear the old folks cry a "Welcome home."
I think I see you sitting by the fire—
The driftwood fire of many a winter's storm—
So safe among us; Think I hear you tell
Of all the winter's perils; of the ice

That kept the good ship prisoner three long months,
And then the fishing of the whales and seals,
The dauntless bravery of all the crew;
With not a word of what yourself had done,
(Albeit you were the bravest of them all,
Always the bravest, truest, dearest, best!)
And now I think I see the old folks rise
To bless us in the firelight; then I feel
The tender heartbeat, and the good-night kiss,
But only till to-morrow at the dawn—
My sailor Eric!
    Why to-day the hours
Seem weeks, while this same day is one long year.
So fast the thoughts fly to the dear life-love,
So slow the feet beat time upon the road
That brings us to it!
    Thus I thought and sang
Among the roses, on that still sweet morn
In our sea-cottage garden by the shore.
Then I remember that the songs and flowers,

The scents and happy feelings, seemed to rise
Together in some fitful, foolish rhyme,
Straight from the heartwells, then a melody
Rushed to my lips, and this is what I sang.

IN THE GARDEN.

Sweet little garden, so full of sweet posies,
    Bloom out your best in the bright-dropping light,
Give her your blossoms, carnations and roses,
    Eric, her sailor, is coming to-night!

Wall-flowers, oh! give her, for Eric, her sailor,
    Dusky brown fragrance he loveth so well;
So it may whisper when spoken words fail her,
    All the dear things that she wishes to tell!

Patch of white clover and greenest of grasses,
    There will she sit in the twilight so sweet,
Happiest woman and blythest of lasses,
    Eric, her sailor love, stretched at her feet.

Ah! little chaffinch, she heareth your singing,
    Knoweth your secret. Your tiny bird-heart
Is beating to be where a soft joy is winging
    Another small chaffinch that flyeth apart!

Bee, your gold honey and flower-rifled treasure
    Boast nothing so lovely as that she shall find
In the heart of her sailor, who loves without measure,
    The heart of her Eric, brave, tender, and kind.

Ope, open pale lily, your pure cup unclosing
    To welcome the sun and the bright-dropping light;
She'll pluck you and wear you, your whiteness reposing
    Against her warm bosom—he cometh to-night.

REALISATION.

The day was nearly over. In the sky
Rocked a white crescent-moon, and one fair star
Gave earnest of the others—Hesperus.
I wearied with the home-tasks and the hours
That moved so slowly, stood beside the fire
Where hummed the cheery kettle. The old folks
Bade me go rest awhile, if rest I could,
Before the night time. "For, sweetheart," they said,
"You know that he would wish to see you bright,
If, by a chance, he comes this summer eve,
And you have been so restless all the day."
So up the stairs I went, and laid me down
A moment on the bed. I think I slept,

I know I dreamt a dream, for never now
There comes another like it. 'Twas the last
In which were mingled life, and hope, and love.
When lo!—I started, for I heard a voice,
A man's, but not our Eric's, *that* I knew
In the half-consciousness of startled sleep.
I rose, and parted on one side the white
Shrouding the lattice windows, leaning out
Only a little.
     Underneath entwined
With honeysuckles creeping, rose the porch;
And there a man was standing, and I knew
That they stood with him listening to his words.
" 'Twas bitter weather, then," I heard him say,
"And Christmas had been gone a good two weeks,
A month we had been ice-bound, and the time
Hung heavy; but they were a cheerful crew.
One day they dragged a boat to where a small
Clear space of sea was running near the berg,
And four got in it. He was watching then

To see that nothing happened, for he felt
Always for others; and they loved him so
In their rough fashion that a single word
Would change their purpose with an 'aye, sir, aye,'
That did your heart good.

     "'Twas a little boat;
And those that manned it rowed with right good will
To make the blood flow in their half-numbed hands.
Perchance they did not keep a good look-out;
But Eric saw behind a sheet of ice
Coming upon the tossing bit of sea
That ran between the bergs on either side.
With that he shouted, and we all ran out,
But not in time—the boat went crashing on
And split in two against the floating mass!
The men were in the water struggling now
For life or death; and he was with them too,
Trying to save them, swimming to the spot
Where the wild waves were bearing fast away
The pieces of the shattered boat; then three

Got hold of them ; the other clutched his arm,
And dragged him under !
     God, it was a sight !
The four were saved—but he, the best, went down.

We searched the whole long day, but never found
A trace of Eric. One of those he died
To help—the man who blindly clutched his arm,
Lived on a week, and in the fever seemed
To know what he had done, for ever cried
' I did not mean it ; wretch and fool I was,'
And so went, raving.
     I was forced to take
The captain's place, and bring the old ship home.

" A fearful thing it was to sail away
And leave him in a frozen unknown sea
Without a Christian burial."

Thus he spoke,
While darker grew the shadows. Then arose
Through all the unreal silence a low cry—
"Oh! who will tell her; who will tell the child?"
And then the world span round. I knew no more.

To-day the winds are freshening from the north,
The angry waves are curling white-capped heads,
Then breaking with a sullen roar upon
The jagged sea-rocks. In the garden now
Lie scattered leaves; the bare boughs overhead
Lace in a stormy sky. They said to me
"Go out a little, for 'twill do you good
To feel the breezes." So I came—and sit
Upon the low stone wall that skirts the shore,
And all the noise of rushing winds and waves
Has woven a song, which, echoing through my brain
Though wild and sad—I cannot choose but sing.

BY THE SEA.

Oh, little bark, that danceth all alone upon the billow!
  What would I give to sail away, to sail away in thee?
To seek, even though for years, and then to find, my Eric's pillow
      In some cold sea!

Oh! wild bird, floating, flying, in the windy, wintry weather;
  Brave sea-bird! darting, sailing, o'er the ocean's sullen dash,
What would I give if you and I could fly away together
      Where icebergs crash?

For, oh! the lonely watches when I keep the candle burning,
 And oh! the lonely dawning when there cometh back the light;
And oh! the lonely day-time, and the lonely twilight turning
   Again to-night!

My Eric! my beloved! I would rather, I would rather
 Sail the frozen seas to find you, where the wild weeds weave your pall;
But I cannot. I am here—and you are there, and God the Father
   Rules over all.

WHY ?

Why?

Was it a kiss too many?
    Was it a word too much,
Than should be kissed and spoken,
    That left the love-tie broken?
Why was it so?   That such
    Should be the fate of any?
              Why?

I only know our days
    Were severed from that hour;
And that some deeper feeling,
    A hidden sense revealing,
Showed where a cloud did lower
    Above our separate ways.
              Why?

Why did we kiss again?
   Why did we smile no more?
While each the other deeming
   Far different than seeming
In those fair days of yore?
   Why did we part in pain?
          Why?

WHICH?

Which?

Love, to our lips, holds up in jewelled glory
    His cup, with life-wine brimming full and high,
Shall we reject or taste? The old, old story,
    Though new to us, my darling—You and I?

Passion cries, "Drink." But pallid wisdom's finger
    Is lifted up in warning. Love, the while,
Tosses the rose-wreathed chalice, as we linger
    Doubting, and mocks us with his sunny smile!

Which shall we choose? To kiss; to weep; to sever;
    Dashing the cup aside with many a sigh—
Or grasp its golden stem—and meet for ever!
    Which shall we choose, my darling?—You and I.

FIAMMETTA.

Fiammetta.

He writes, the old man, in the lonely Grange.

This is her picture.   Every day I twine
Fresh garlands round it with weak agèd hands;
My old dim eyes, which gaze through unshed tears,
Drink in her beauty, dear at once, and strange.
My Fiammetta! how thy southern sun
Gleams in the velvet darkness of thine eyes!
And how the pallid brightness of the north
Shines in the amber clusters of thy hair!

Half English, half Italian, lo! she came
From her sweet south to our dull leaden skies,

A distant cousin from a distant land,
To gladden all the household with her voice,
Her bright swift glances; for, until she came,
No woman reigned within the dull old Grange.

He, my half-brother, loved her, for herself,
For her quick graces, for the nameless all
That goes to make a woman's gentleness;
But, dumb with love, he dared not speak the word,
Asking for what he longed for. So, one day,
Seeing his trouble, her unconsciousness
Vexed me (albeit I felt a pang
Drag at my heart-strings),
      And I spoke to her.

My library is full of old oak chairs
And writing-tables, and a sombre hue

Clothes the dark walls from dusky lines of books.
She, entering, cast a light on all around,
Reflected from her simple dress of white,
And from the falling fragrance of her curls.
I drew her to the seat whereon I sat,
And—" Pretty cousin, I would speak with you "—
When, with a startled glance, her southern eyes
Flashed into mine, and quick I hurried on—
" My cousin, since you came to this dull home,
Like light to darkness, you have made us glad;
But have you never guessed the love he bears—
My soldier brother—and the pain he feels
To part with you holding his inmost heart,
For, this day week, he leaves us.
     He is dumb,
Because he fears your answer; seeing which
I must speak for him. Tell me, could you love
And follow him as wife?"
     Again that glance,
With its strange question, sought my troubled face.

And I went on—

     "Full twenty years I count,
Upon my wrinkled forehead, more than he.
You cannot choose but love him, young and brave,
Handsome as an Apollo!

     Speak my child,
I, who might be your father, counsel you,
If you can love him—love him."

     Turning round,
I looked full at her. With averted face
She stood. A low wind coming from the wood,
Through the wide-opened window, stirred the leaves
Of an old book I held, and sighed among
The scattered papers on my writing-desk.

Then through the waiting silence she broke forth,
Wringing her tiny hands and weeping sore,
Like some hot thunderstorm of her own land—

"And you," she cried, "and you to counsel me
To this same marriage, you to ask it—you!
Then, as I sat amazed, she turned and went.

I listened to the little feet which beat
So softly on the carpet, till the door
Opened and shut, and then I laid my head
Upon my ancient desk; for oh! I knew
That with love's wild despair I loved her too,
And all the thought of what the boy might say,
That he might think I falsely had betrayed
His secret to my own advantage.   When
Slowly the door unclosed again, and two
Soft rounded arms were laid about my neck;
A sweet voice whispered low into my ear,
In broken English (she could never learn
Our language perfectly).
     'Twas thus she spoke—
" Forgive me, cousin; there are times in life

When woman's dignity must bend and bow,
Or else the heart breaks! Is it you are blind,
Or only cruel, that you take me now
And give me to another? You I love.
I say it. You are angry. I shall die."

Oh! Fiammetta, always my heart's queen!

He sailed away in autumn. In the spring
He came again to visit the old house,
And found it empty of all blessedness.

Her hand shall never touch embroidery more,
The walls shall never echo to her tread;
Her step is silent in the old oak halls,
No singing music on the hushed air falls;
Only her picture resteth.
                She is dead!

MARY LEE.

Mary Lee.

She stood beside him on the yellow sands,
    A sweeter Cornish lass there could not be ;
A low mist hung, a misty moon hung low,
    Above the yellow sands that skirt the sea.
        He was an Earldom's heir, and she
        A fisher's daughter—Mary Lee.

The sleeping village right behind them lay,
    The church clock slowly struck the hour of ten ;
Her cheek was pressed to his all wet with tears,
    And oh ! how sadly was he sighing then—
        " I cannot part, my own, from thee,
        I cannot leave thee—Mary Lee.

What care I for the busy heartless world!
    I've wooed, I'll claim thee for my fair young bride;
And we will be so happy in our love,
    And live and die together side by side!
        I must, I will, be true to thee,
            My one heart's darling, Mary Lee."

Her father in the little alehouse sat,
    And when he heard the tolling hour of ten;
He drained the last drops left within his glass
    Then rose, and nodded to the other men.
        "Good night," he said, "she waits for me,
            My little daughter—Mary Lee!"

Beside the fire her would-be lover stood,
    Black-browed and scowling, tall was he and strong;
Long laughed he out as scornfully he gazed,
    Stalwart the stalwart fishermen among.
        "You think she waits at home," sneered he,
            Your pretty daughter—Mary Lee!"

"I saw them both not half-an-hour ago
    Down on the shore, his arm was round her waist;
I watched them kiss again, and once again—
    Your little daughter! Yes. The Earl has taste."
        Another laugh. A madman he
        Who ran to seek sweet Mary Lee.

Damp dews lay on her uncurled chestnut hair,
    The last kiss given, the misty moonlight fell
Around them as they turned to go; when there
    Rushed Lee, his eyes on fire, his heart a hell.
        But calmly by the sobbing sea,
        She turned to meet him—Mary Lee.

"Father!" she said, but he, half blind with rage
    Ran onwards towards the Earl, a knife gleamed high;
"Take that," he hissed, and hurled it through the air,
    Then rose a fearful shriek—a woman's cry,
        For ere the Earl could turn to flee,
        Across his breast fell Mary Lee.

An instant in the dim and misty light
    Glittered the blade. With white arms stretched apart
As if to shield him, stood the poor girl there,
    And took the knife into her brave young heart,
        Then fell, and died beside the sea,
        To save her lover—Mary Lee.

They say at midnight, on the yellow sands,
    When mists rise, and when misty moons hang low;
With bright dishevelled hair, and folded hands
    Clasping a knife-blade—you may see her go.
        I know not if such things can be,
        But this is what they tell to me,
        Who knew and loved poor Mary Lee.

AMOR MORTUUS.

Amor Mortuus.

Long years ago, when all the world was young
    And fresh and sweet, one morning I espied
Love standing by my side.
    White, sun-kissed lilies in his hand;
With these he smote my heart-door, as he cried,
    "Open, at Love's command."
And lo! my heart-door on its hinges swung
        And slowly opened wide.

Love entered; all my life seemed fair and gay.
    With passion's blossoms rare my heart he dressed,
My lips with kisses pressed.
    A thousand times I would that I had died
Ere I had opened to the Vision blessed!
    Ah! would I had denied
The stranger welcome; for one bitter day
        He died within my breast.

AMOR MORTUUS.

Love lieth dead; for ever pale and still
    By cruel hands, false vows, all foully slain,
Red with his life-blood's stain.
    No lilies now, or passion-blooms he bears,
Only the thorny crimson rose of pain
    Upon his breast he bears.
I kiss his trailing wings and lips so chill,
        I weep—I call, in vain.

Shall there, in some far day—some unborn year,
    Some yet unwelcomed hour, undreamt before,
A step pause by my door?
    A hand smite on the portal closed so fast,
A Voice, that thrills my being to its core,
    Bid my Love rise at last?
Or shall he, in eternal silence drear
        Lie dead for evermore?

SONG.

Song.

My Love who loves me not.

A bouquet for my love who loves me not!
    What shall I gather? Rich, dark roses, set
In thorns, ah me! like love? Or lilies fair?
    Tall, bloodless lily-blooms; or violets wet
And sweet with night-dews or carnations rare?
               And yet—
White poppy-buds were best that teach one to
    forget.

A song for my dear love, who loves me not!
   Sing, blackbird, thrilling in yon leafy brake.
Coo, cushat, coo. Chant, thrush, thy sweetest
   strain.
   Thou nightingale, with passionate throbbings, wake
Pain in her heart, who heeds not of my pain,
        And make
Her pity me, who die for her sweet sake.

TWIN SOULS.

Twin Souls.

Some kindly look, some undefined expression
    Lurks in the shadow of thy earnest eyes ;
Some secret thing which claims my heart's possession
        By sympathetic ties.

Some likeness of the mind, some fellow-feeling,
    Blends our cleft lives to one harmonious whole.
'Thy good unto my better self appealing
        Haunts all my inmost soul.

Wordless—yet ever to my thoughts replying,
    Giving me look for look, and breath for breath,
With thee—the world is paradise undying,
        Without thee—Life is Death.

MOONLIGHT ON COMO.

Moonlight on Como.

'Tis midnight now; and all the breezes here
    Make one faint breeze which rocks my tiny boat
Over the lake, while pallid moonlight clear
    Shimmers above my bark as on I float.

Fair sleeps the light upon the sleeping flowers,
    And sleeping villages, half up the hill,
Where Rest has laid her hand. And all the hours
    Of busy day at length are hushed and still.

I only, gazing at the gazing stars,
    Drink in the heavenly beauty of the night;
Bathed in the moonbeams—dreaming, nothing mars
    The perfect sense of stillness and delight.

This is enchantment. All the earth is naught,
   All others are not; only I alone
Feel the true peace, the quietude oft sought
   Rocking amid the water's undertone.

No one is here to tear with ruthless hand
   The magic from my ears by echoed speech,
Whose soul my soul can never understand,
   Whose heart my half-said words can never reach.

Only a nightingale, whose sobbing song
   Floods on the moonlight, seeming in its strain
To wake to tears a heart that once did long
   In other hearts to find itself again.

Alone! 'Tis but a type of life's lone way,
   'Mid all the waves of light and melody,
To feel to-morrow, now, and yesterday
   Solve not the riddle or the mystery.

There is no perfect peace in this unrest,
    To-night is but a shadow of " to be,"
Where separate souls, with longings long suppressed,
    Shall mingle in a single harmony.

Ah! these my thoughts have stolen from the night
    Too much of darkness; see the sinking moon
Behind the mountain dips, and fades from sight,
    Leaving the stars and me alone too soon.

Fair sleep the roses. Halfway up the hill
    The villages are slumb'ring. Here I float
Alone upon the waters, on—until
    The breeze shall cease to drift my tiny boat.

THE LOVE BIRD.

The Love Bird.

A love-bird came to the window pane,
   His song was sweet and clear;
Ever again the strange refrain
   Fell on my listening ear—
      "Tweet, tweet! look up, my sweet;
        Your love is near!"

"Ah, but my love is far away,
   Sailing the summer sea;
Many a weary night and day
   Must pass ere he come to me.
      Peace, peace, love-bird, and cease;
        It cannot be!"

He only shook his golden wings;
    His song rose loud and clear,
As if he knew and heard the things
    I could not know and hear.
        "Tweet, tweet! look up, my sweet;
            Your love is near!"

"Ah! but my heart is full of tears,
    My life of misery;
My nights are haunted by the fears
    Of winds, and waves, and sea.
        "Away, away, love-bird, I say,
            It is not he."

A step, a climbing up the stair—
    Whose voice is this I hear?
The love-bird shook his pinions there;
    And, ah! his song thrilled clear—
        "Tweet, tweet; look up, my sweet;
            Your love is here!"

A PERFECT DAY.

A Perfect Day.

We went together up the side
   Of some far hill, on that far day;
Where, in the grass, clear streamlets glide;
   Where flickering shadows softly play.
              Ah, me!
That this should be but one long memory.

A brook was singing in the sun,
   As if it strove our lips to teach
Some secret of its water's run—
   Some words that scarce find sound in speech.
              And so
We drank love's cup, and listened to its flow.

My sweet—we lingered near the stream
    Till melting gold turned all to grey;
And now it only seems a dream—
    The memory of that perfect day.
            Thus pass
Love's hours, like breath-stains breathed upon a glass.

LUX ET TENEBRAE.

G

Lux et Tenebrae.

There was a time when hope was all mine own;
    There was an hour when love and life were mine;
There was a day when summer's sweetest sun
        Was mine and thine.

But hope has withered into wild regret,
    And love and life are buried, ruined, gone—
A grave hath opened, and the sun hath set
        On me alone.

Then, when I think of thee, all death is dark;
    Then, when I dream of thee, all life is light.
How shall I launch my soul-boat, fragile bark,
        In unknown night?

How shall I, straining, catch with dying ears
    Thy last loved accents from that other shore?
How shall my eyes meet thine through blinding tears?
        I see no more.

When I forget thee, then I would not rob
    My heart of peace which death alone can give!
When I remember—comes a passionate throb—
        I long to live!

FROM THE ITALIAN OF
STECCHETTI.

From the Italian of Stecchetti.

'Twas winter, late, and close beside the fire,
    Alone, embarrassed, sat we there together,
Like two school-fellows, with the same desire,
    Yet blushing as we talked about the weather.

On her embroidery her eyes were bent,
    Mine to the vaulted ceiling I was raising ;
Seeming to see not, yet quick glances went
    Far better, perhaps, than if we had been gazing !

I thought, "I'd give, for one sweet smile of grace,
Of my poor talents all the flowers most rare,
All the young blood which in my veins doth flow,"

When she, uprising, turning pale of face,
Caught her two little hands among my hair,
And "Listen," whispered soft, "I love you so!"

AFTER STECCHETTI.

After Stecchetti.

A bitter night.
    I cannot sleep for all the rain and sleet
    Dashing against the panes ; along the street
Whistles the wind.
    The mad, wild winter wind, with horrid shriek,
    The answering trees respond with groan and
        creak.
The watch-dogs howl.
    I hear, as tossing on my bed I lie,
    Borne on the air, a sudden wailing cry,
A wailing cry.—

AFTER STECCHETTI.

From my lone pillow then I lift my head,
And listen to the voice of one long dead.
'Tis thine, poor ghost!
Behind thy marble door thou canst not rest,
Until thy head is pillowed on my breast.
Within thy tomb,
With folded hands, with pallid, lifeless tress,
Thou waitest ever for my love caress!
Hush! I shall come.
Dead hands shall knock, dead hands shall ope the door;
And dead, by dead, lie dead for evermore.

SOMEWHERE.

Somewhere.

A POET'S IDEAL.

Ah! did you see her there?
    In her pearly-tinted dress,
  Brushing back the hollow grasses
  With little feet, that press
    So lightly as she passes.
        Say, did you see her there?

Ah! did you meet her there?
    Like a glory-crown her hair,
  Like a saintly aureole;
  And her eyes are shining fair
    With the fair thoughts of her soul.
        Say, did you meet her there?

Ah! did you see her there?
    All the woodland birds are still,
And swing, as keeping time
In the boughs, to her sweet thrill—
    Swing, as keeping time and rhyme.
        Say, did you see her there!

Ah! did you meet her there?
    The sunset, flickering, flashes
Through the leaves to where she stands,
Throwing scintillating dashes
    On her little claspèd hands.
        Say, did you meet her there?

I have never seen her yet,
Never found my fair dream-maiden,
White-robed, standing in the grasses,
Standing in the golden wood;
With her dewy eyes love-laden,
Singing, 'mid a yellow flood

Of the sunlight. She is there.
I shall reach her unaware
(For I know that she is there),
I shall touch her as she passes ;
She shall stay at love's commands,
And, at last, among the grasses
We shall join our parted hands.
When the sun has scarcely set,
Somewhere—I shall find her yet.

AFTER MANY DAYS.

After Many Days.

How many days have dawned ; and suns have set
And risen ; and how many winter snows
Have fallen ; and how many stormy blasts
Have lashed the ocean into mighty waves,
And swept the deserts ; and how many moons
Have climbed the summer skies, and shed their light
On peaceful homesteads and on sleeping hills,
And valleys black with shadows—since we met?

How swiftly flies on Time, when outstretched hands
Of happy ones would hold him ; and how slow
Drag his dread moments over fettered souls !
So, in the shadows, as I sit and write,
The days I write of seem a summer's dream,
Dreamt in the early sunlight of a morn

While song-birds twittered near the window-pane,
And roses bloomed—and all the world was fair.
But, ah! the waking; and the long long years
That followed on that waking; and the hours
That crept, lead-weighted, o'er our empty lives.

It seemed a dream. And yet it lasted days,
Or months, or years—for love can count no time.
I, who now write upon this senseless sheet,
Thrill, as I write, with memories—nothing more.
And you, who may perchance some other day
Take up this sheet and read it, *you* will thrill
With these same memories, when you see my words.

There was a gulf between us, narrow, so
That we clasped hands above it; and a step
Could span it; but 'twas deep and dark as death.
Only we heeded not, and thought no wrong
Or danger in the sweetness of the hour
Till one sad day.

You drew me half across
And, in a startled moment, sealed my lips
With a long love-kiss. 'Twas the first, the last.
For then I felt the earth beneath my feet
Tremble and rock. A gleam of sunlight showed
Just for a moment, all the dread abyss
Between us; and the horror of the depth
Seen for a second only—held us dumb.

We could not span it, but with broken vows;
We could not cross but with dishonoured feet.
And, for true hearts, 'twere better loss or death
Than faithless faith, and honour in the dust.

And so—we parted.

And the little gulf
That cleft us lies between us to this day.

But there will come a time when we can meet;
When all the sorrows borne and duties done

Shall twine a wreath around our conquering brows—
For he is greatest who has conquered even
Himself for honour.

    We shall meet again.
And, clasping hands across the narrow gulf,
Shall feel a higher love, and passion's wave
Shall cease to trouble.

    We shall be at peace.
And, in that day, remember as of old
Each other's aspirations, and the thoughts
Lying too deep for words in kindred souls.
So, standing thus apart, on either side,
The days shall pass.

     At last an hour shall come
When one shall throw a bridge across the gulf,
On which to cross and meet for evermore,
For he shall span it o'er whose name is Death.

www.ingramcontent.com/pod-product-compliance
Lightning Source LLC
Chambersburg PA
CBHW020143170426
43199CB00010B/860